EASY PIANO

MAROON 5

ISBN 978-1-4950-5040-4

HAL•LEONARD®
CORPORATION
7777 W. BLUEMOUND RD. P.O. BOX 13819 MILWAUKEE, WI 53213

Visit Hal Leonard Online at

ANIMALS

Words and Music by ADAM LEVINE,
BEN LEVIN and SHELLBACK

Moderately

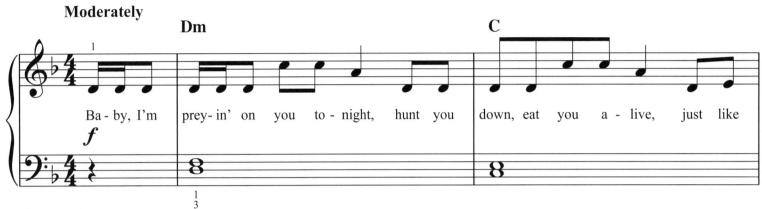

Ba - by, I'm prey-in' on you to-night, hunt you down, eat you a - live, just like

an - i - mals, _ an - i - mals, _ like an - i - mals - mals. _ May - be you

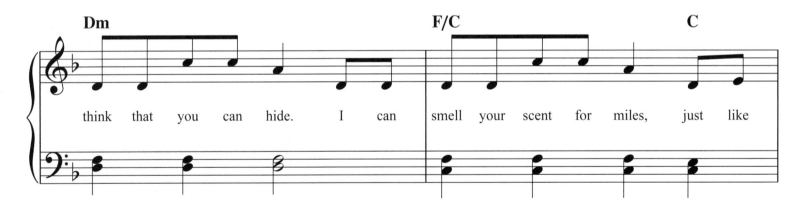

think that you can hide. I can smell your scent for miles, just like

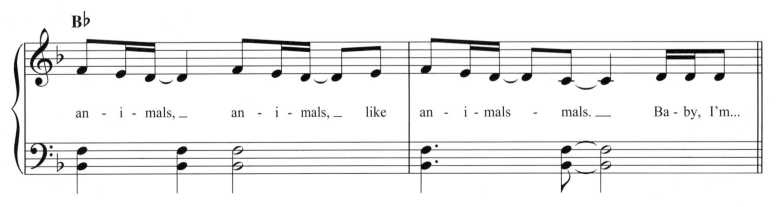

an - i - mals, _ an - i - mals, _ like an - i - mals - mals. _ Ba - by, I'm...

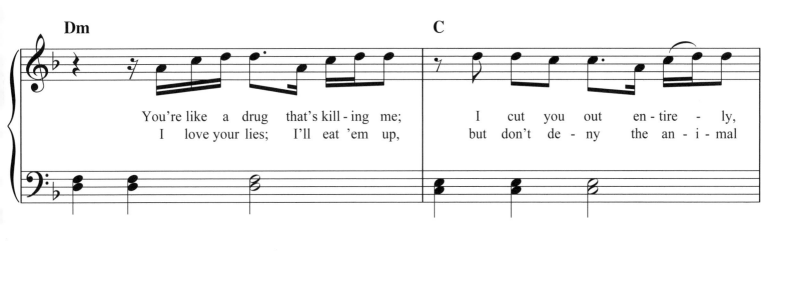

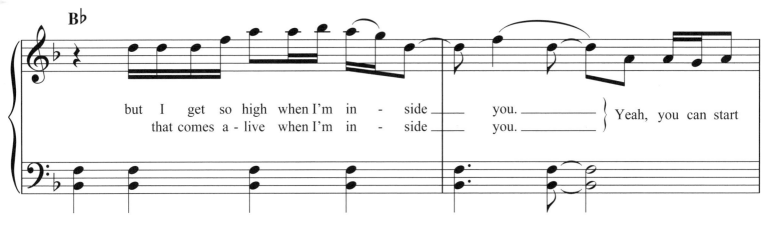

o - ver, you can run free, you can find oth - er fish in the sea. You can pre -

tend it's meant to be; but you can't stay a - way from me. I can still

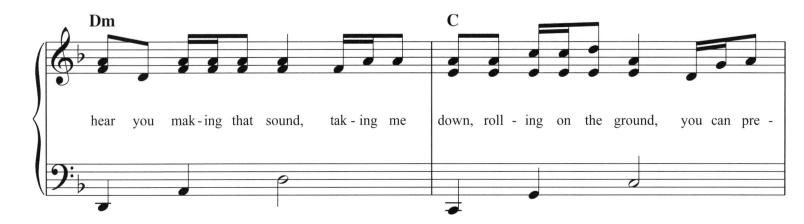

hear you mak - ing that sound, tak - ing me down, roll - ing on the ground, you can pre -

tend that it was me, but no. ____ Oh, ____ ba - by, I'm

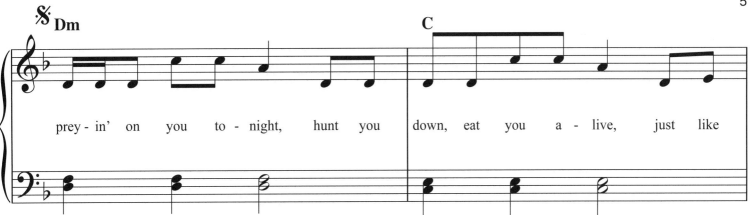

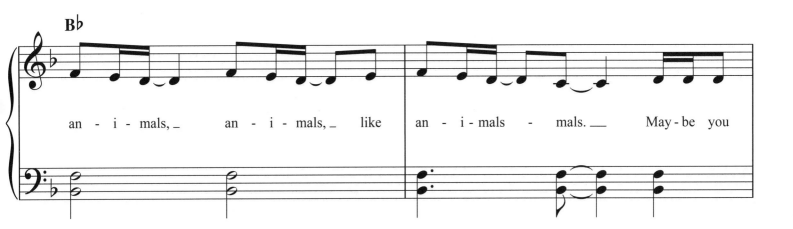

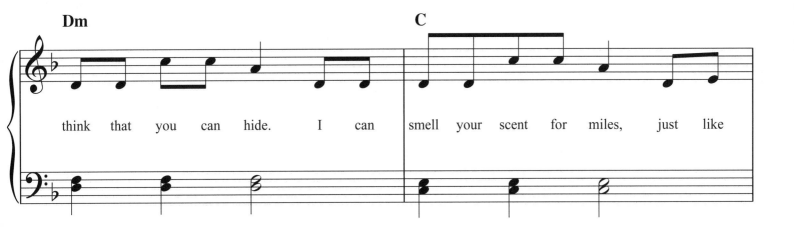

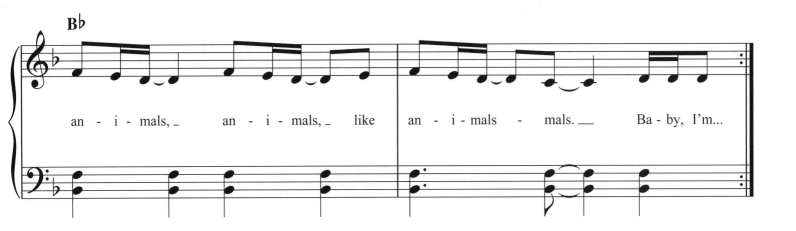

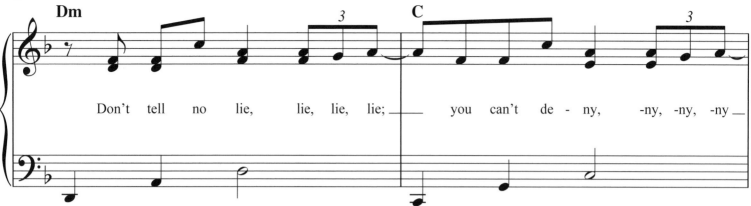

Don't tell no lie, lie, lie, lie; __ you can't de - ny, -ny, -ny, -ny __

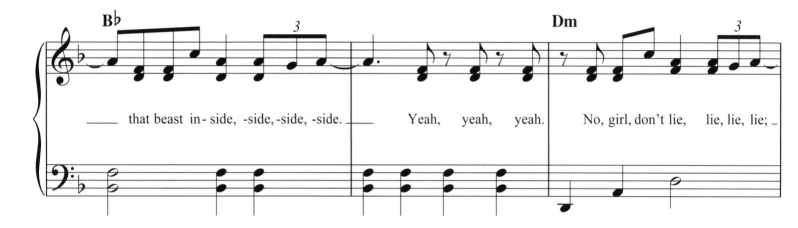

__ that beast in - side, -side, -side, -side. __ Yeah, yeah, yeah. No, girl, don't lie, lie, lie, lie; _

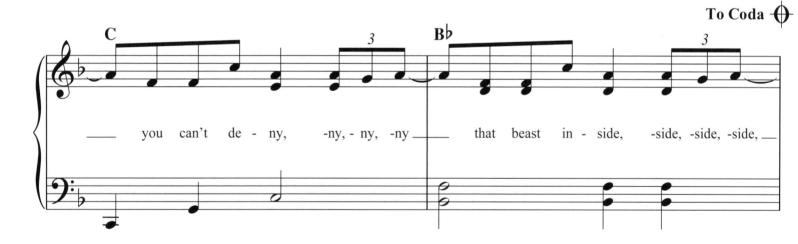

__ you can't de - ny, -ny, - ny, -ny __ that beast in - side, -side, -side, -side, __

To Coda ⊕

D.S. al Coda

__ yeah. __ Ba - by, I'm

CODA ⊕

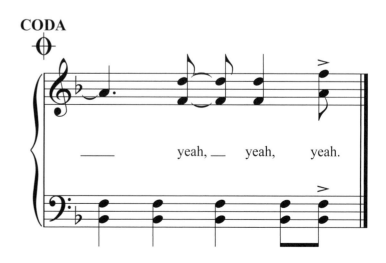

__ yeah, __ yeah, yeah.

MISERY

Words by ADAM LEVINE
Music by ADAM LEVINE, JESSE CARMICHAEL
and SAM FARRAR

Moderate Funk Rock groove

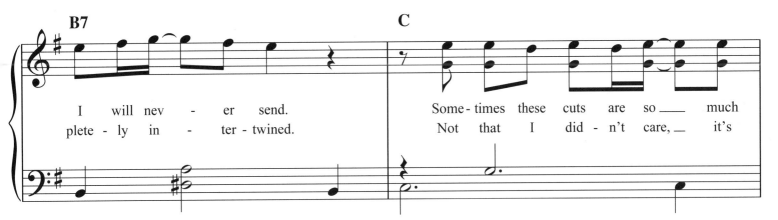

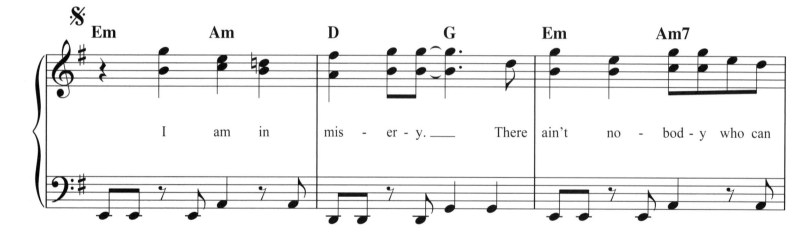

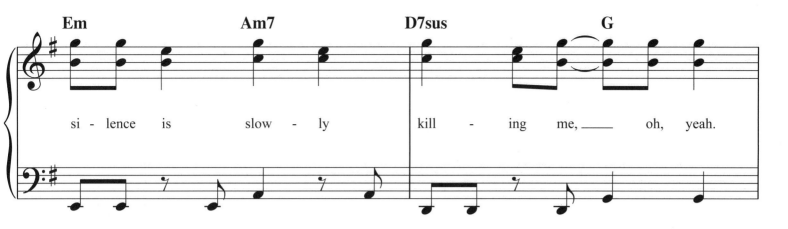

si - lence is slow - ly kill - ing me, ____ oh, yeah.

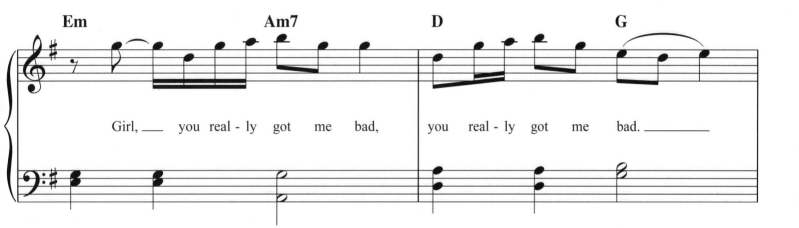

Girl, ___ you real - ly got me bad, you real - ly got me bad. ____

I'm ___ gon - na get you back, I'm gon - na get you back, yeah.

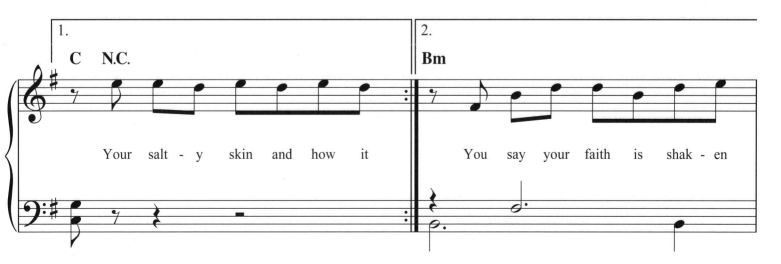

1.
Your salt - y skin and how it

2.
You say your faith is shak - en

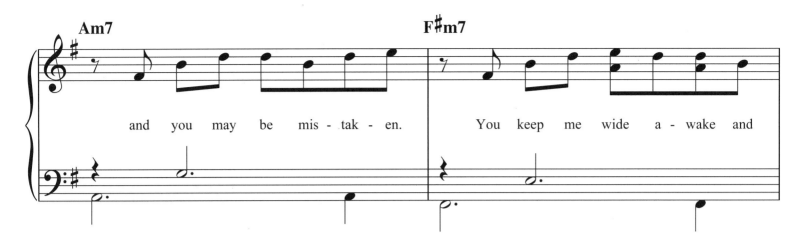

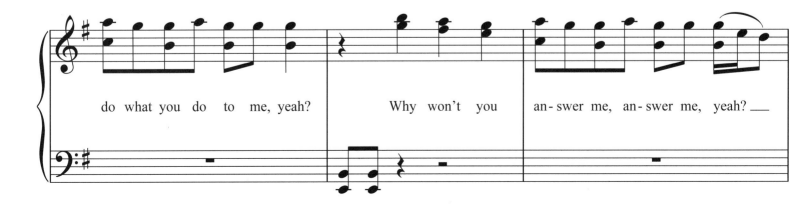

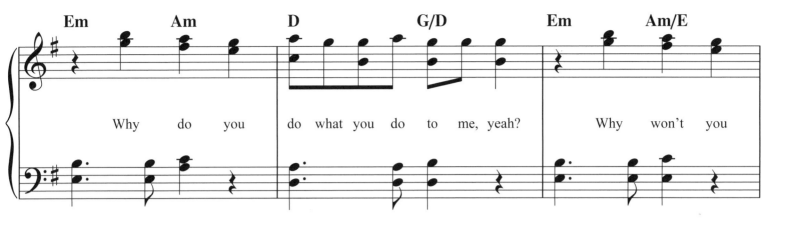

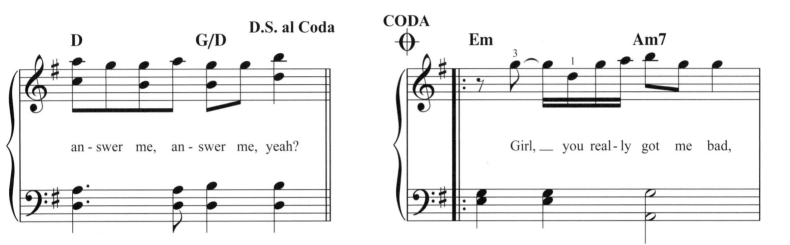

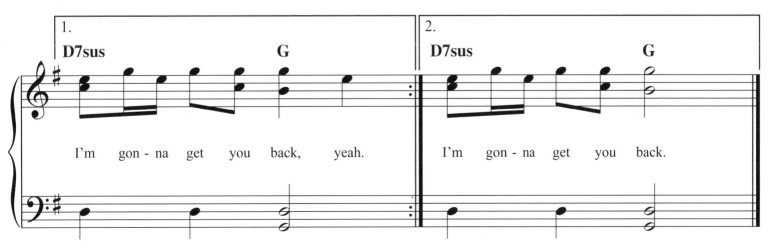

DAYLIGHT

Words and Music by ADAM LEVINE,
MAX MARTIN, SAM MARTIN
and MASON LEVY

With energy

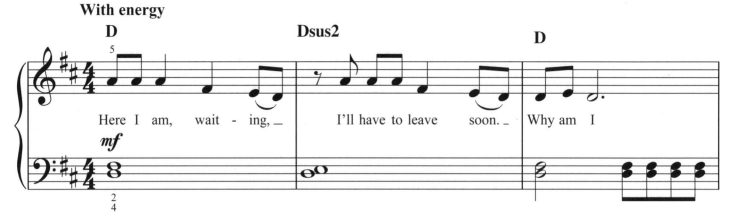

Here I am, wait-ing, I'll have to leave soon. Why am I

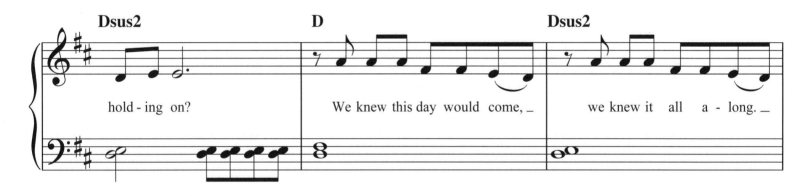

hold-ing on? We knew this day would come, we knew it all a-long.

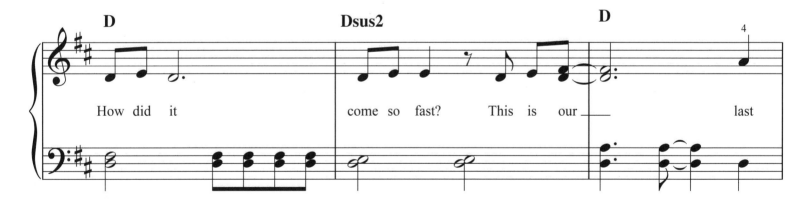

How did it come so fast? This is our last

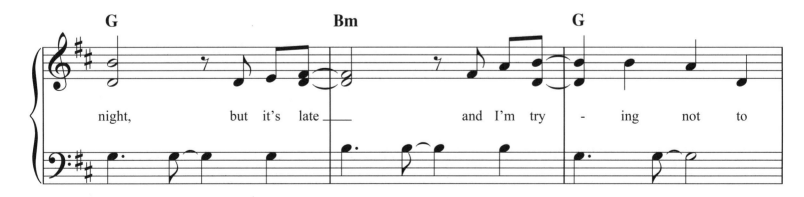

night, but it's late and I'm try-ing not to

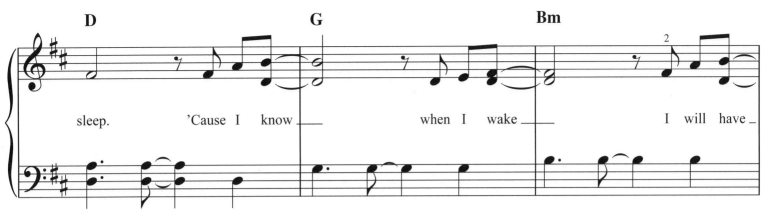

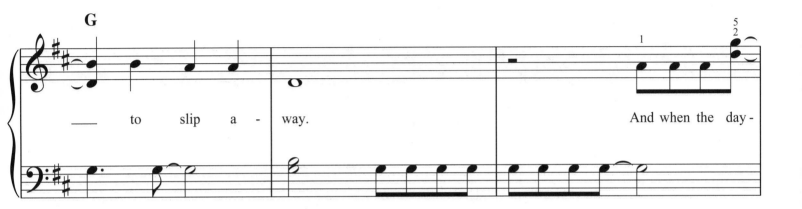

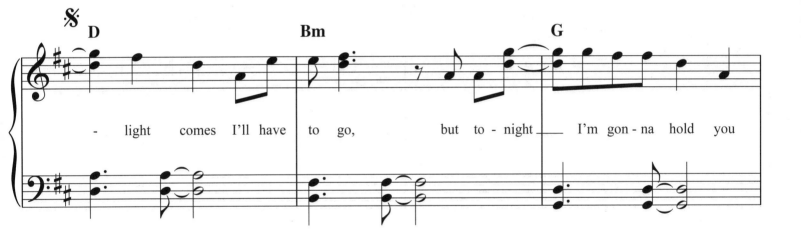

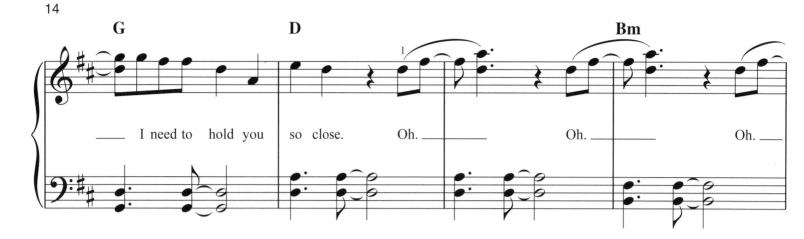

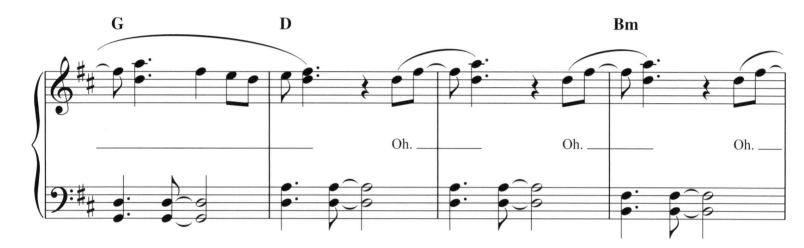

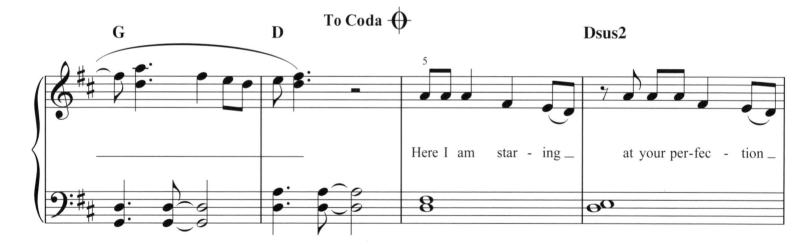

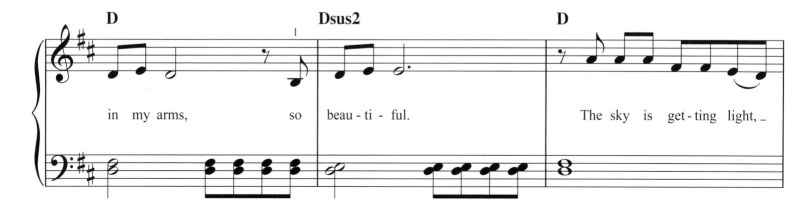

15

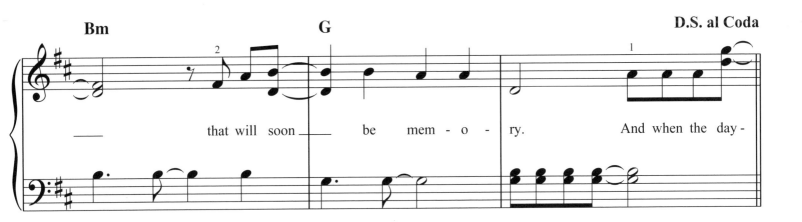

CODA

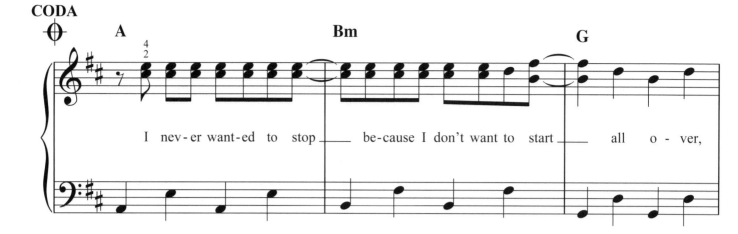

I nev-er want-ed to stop_____ be-cause I don't want to start_____ all o - ver,

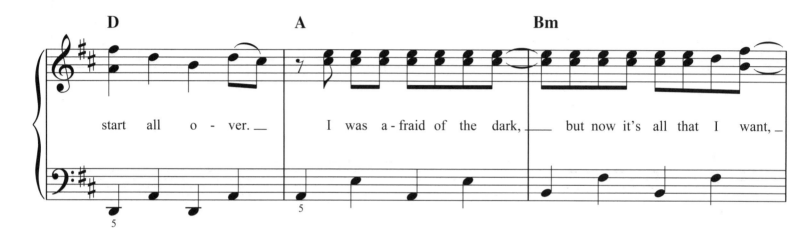

start all o - ver.___ I was a-fraid of the dark,___ but now it's all that I want,___

___ all that I want, all that I want.___ And when the day -

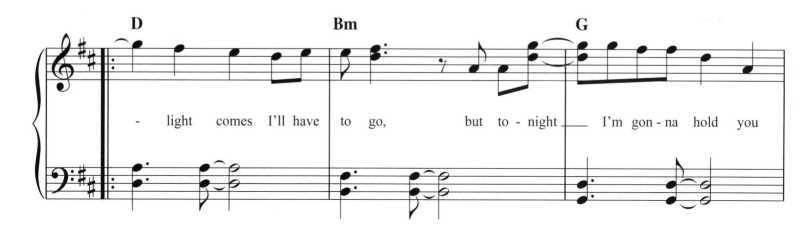

- light comes I'll have to go, but to-night___ I'm gon-na hold you

so close. 'Cause in the day - light we'll be on our own, but to - night _

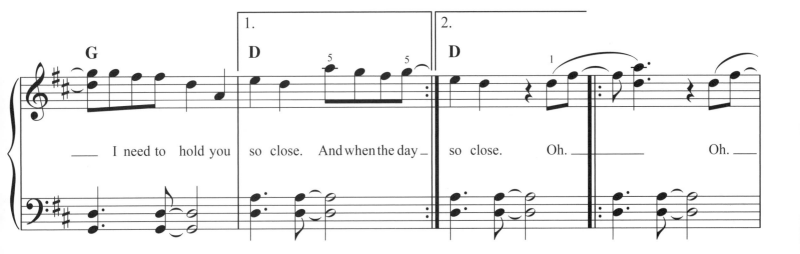

_ I need to hold you so close. And when the day _ so close. Oh. _ Oh. _

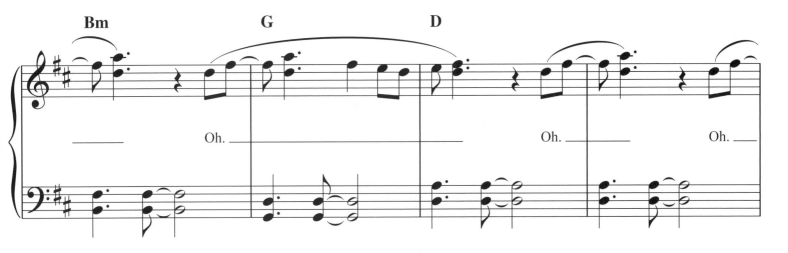

_ Oh. _ Oh. _ Oh.

_ Oh. _ Oh. _

LOVE SOMEBODY

Words and Music by ADAM LEVINE,
NATHANIEL MOTTE, RYAN TEDDER
and NOEL ZANCANELLA

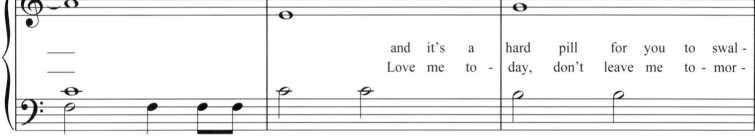

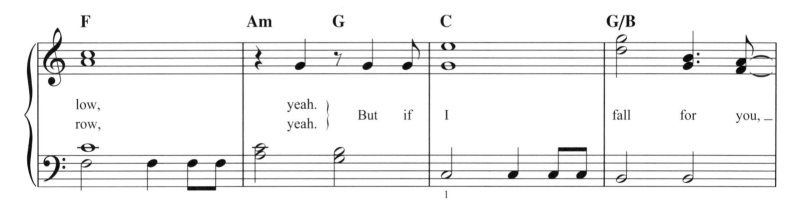

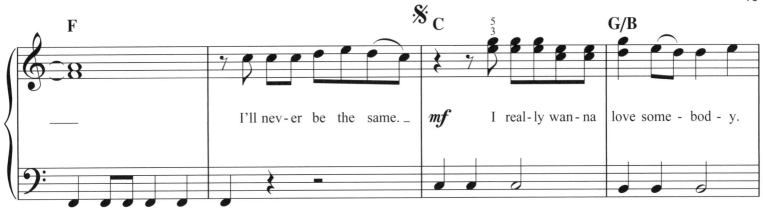

Am **G** **C** **G**

ev - 'ry sin - gle day. ___ I know we're on - ly half - way ___ there, but you can

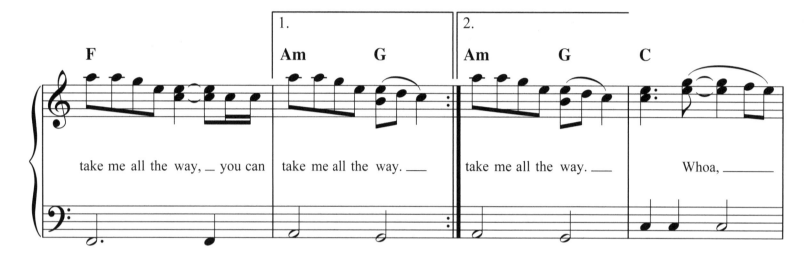

F | 1. **Am** **G** | 2. **Am** **G** **C**

take me all the way, ___ you can | take me all the way. ___ | take me all the way. ___ Whoa, ___

To Coda ⊕

G/B **F** **Am** **G** **C**

whoa, ___ whoa, ___ oh, oh, ___ oh. Whoa, ___

G/B **F** **Am** **G** **C**

whoa, ___ whoa, ___ oh, oh, ___ oh. I don't know where to start,

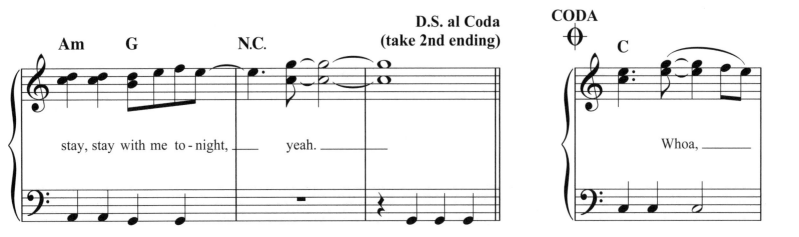

MAKES ME WONDER

Words by ADAM LEVINE
Music by ADAM LEVINE,
JESSE CARMICHAEL and MICKEY MADDEN

Moderately fast

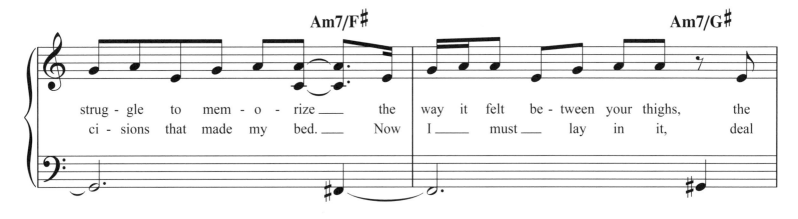

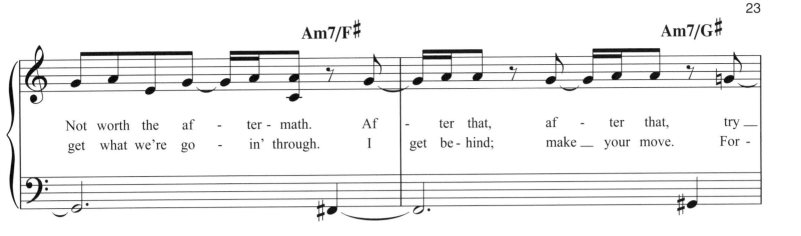

don't be-lieve in you an-y - more, an-y - more.____ I won-der if it

1.
e - ven makes a dif - f'rence to try.____ Yeah, so this is good - bye.

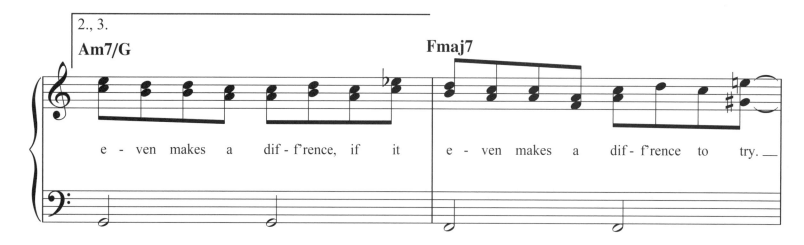

2., 3.
e - ven makes a dif - f'rence, if it e - ven makes a dif - f'rence to try. ___

___ And it's all 'bout how you feel it, but I

don't be - lieve it's true an - y - more, an - y - more._____ I won - der if it

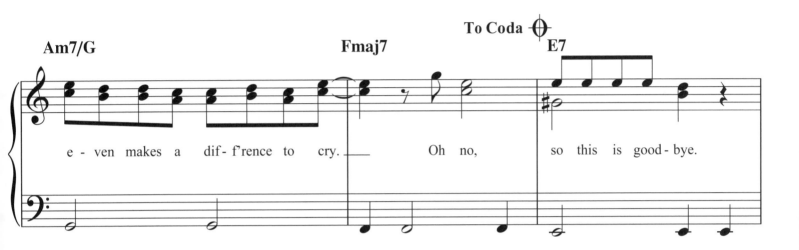

e - ven makes a dif - f'rence to cry.____ Oh no, so this is good - bye.

And I've been here be - fore. One day I'll wake up and it won't hurt an - y - more.__

_____ You caught me in a lie; I have no al - i - bi.

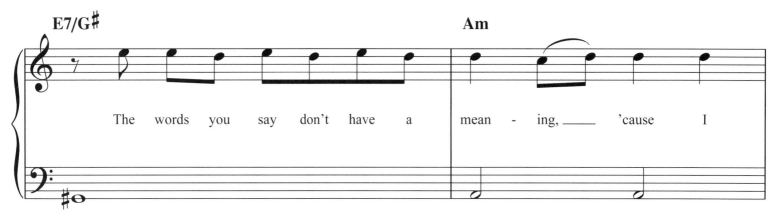

The words you say don't have a mean - ing, ___ 'cause I

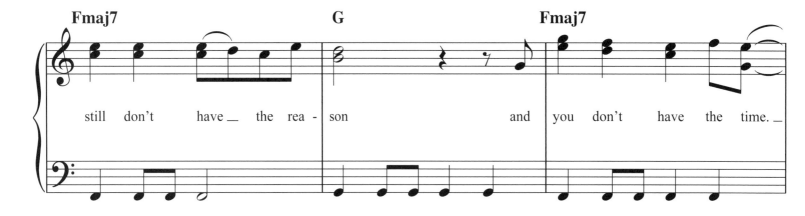

still don't have ___ the rea - son and you don't have the time. ___

___ And it real - ly makes me won - der if I

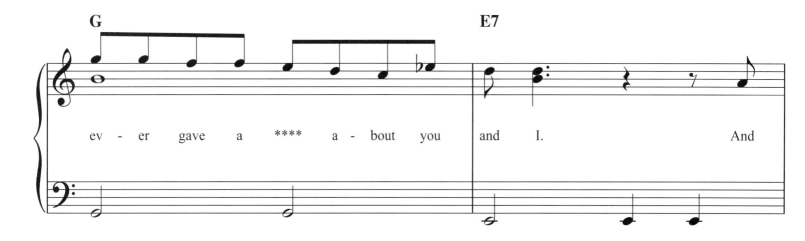

ev - er gave a **** a - bout you and I. And

D.S. al Coda
(take 2nd ending)

so this is good - bye. _____   Give me some - thing to be - lieve in, 'cause I

CODA

so this is good - bye. _____   So this is good - bye. _____

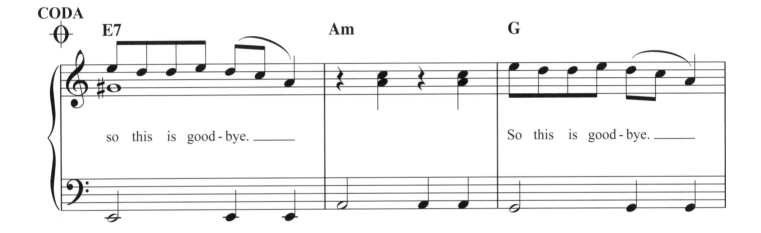

Yeah,   so this is good - bye. _____   Yeah,

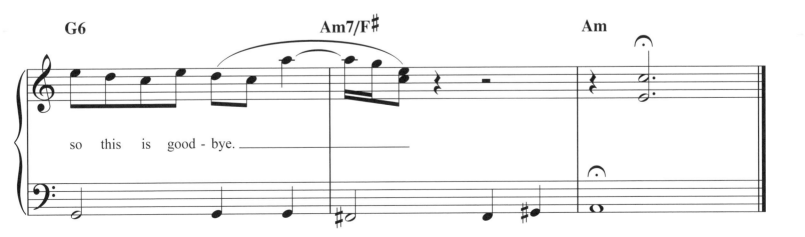

so this is good - bye. _____

MOVES LIKE JAGGER

Words and Music by ADAM LEVINE,
BENJAMIN LEVIN, AMMAR MALIK
and JOHAN SCHUSTER

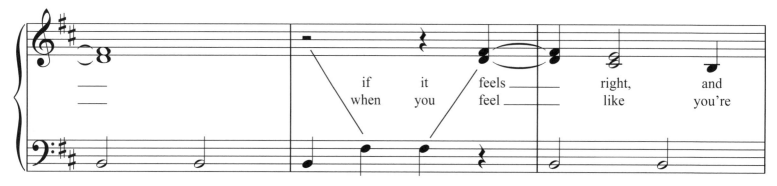

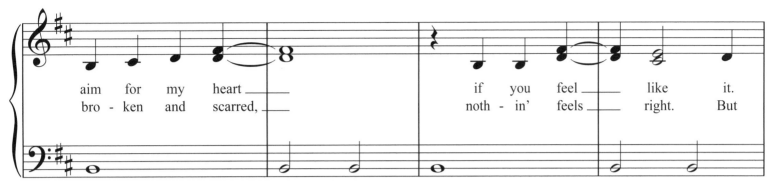

aim for my heart _____ if you feel _____ like it.
bro - ken and scarred, _____ noth - in' feels _____ right. But

Em7

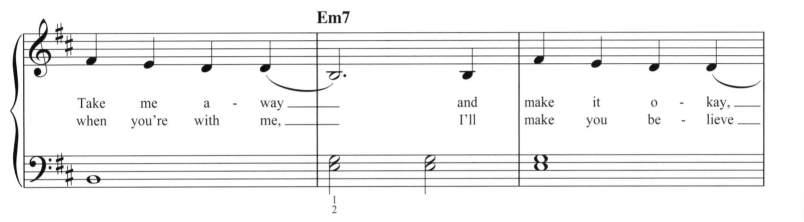

Take me a - way _____ and make it o - kay, _____
when you're with me, _____ I'll make you be - lieve _____

I swear I'll be - have.
that I've got the key.

Bm

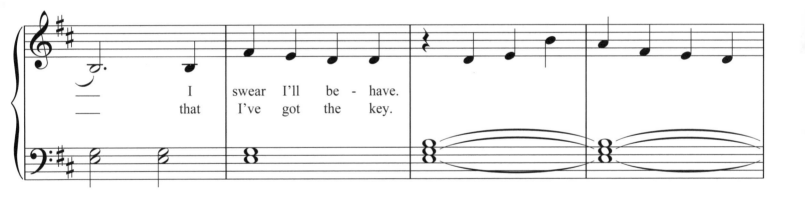

You want - ed con - trol, _____
So get in the car, _____

30

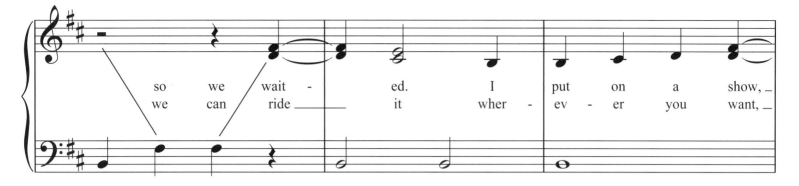

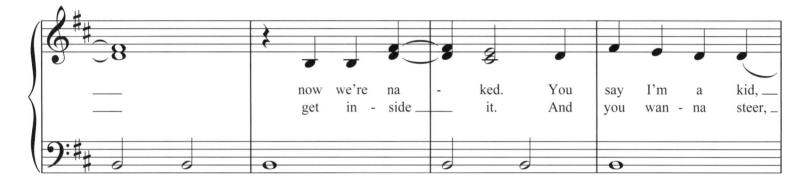

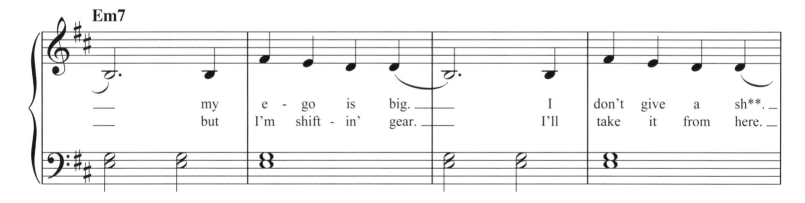

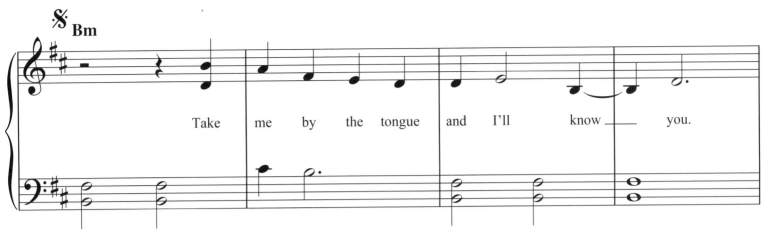

Take me by the tongue and I'll know _____ you.

Kiss me 'til you're drunk and I'll show _____ you all the

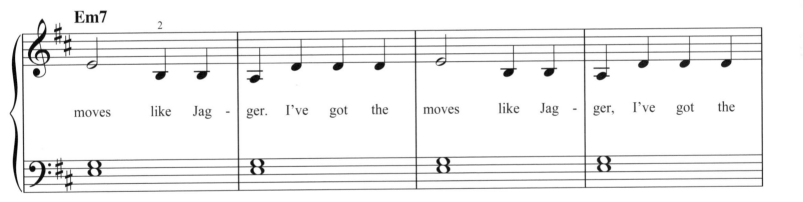

moves like Jag - ger. I've got the moves like Jag - ger, I've got the

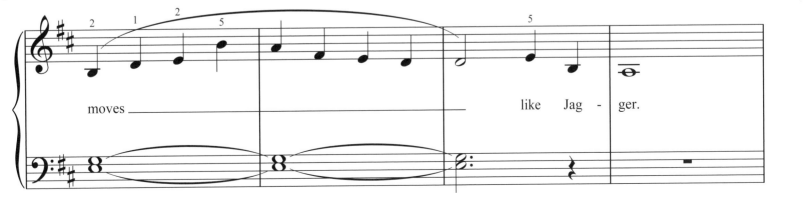

moves _____ like Jag - ger.

I don't need to try to con - trol _____ you.

Look in - to my eyes and I'll own _____ you with them

moves like Jag - ger. I've got the moves like Jag -

ger, I've got the moves. _____

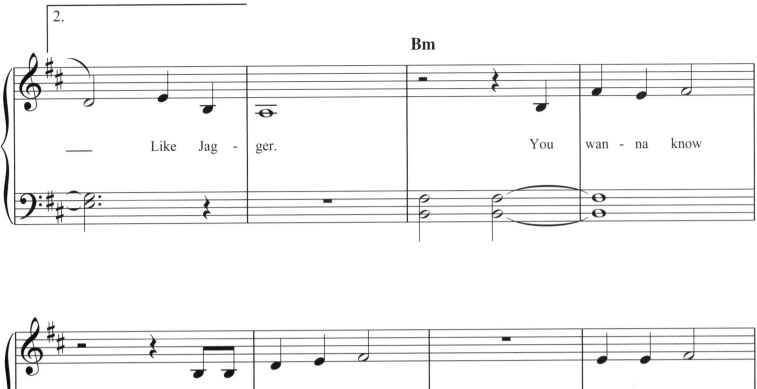

Bm

Like Jag - ger.   You wan - na know

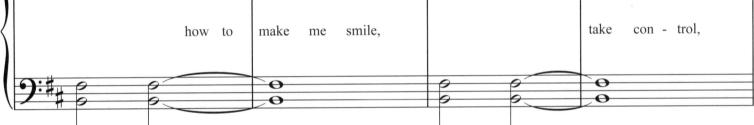

how to make me smile,   take con - trol,

Em7

own me just for the night.   But if I

share my se - cret,   you're gon - na have to keep it. ___

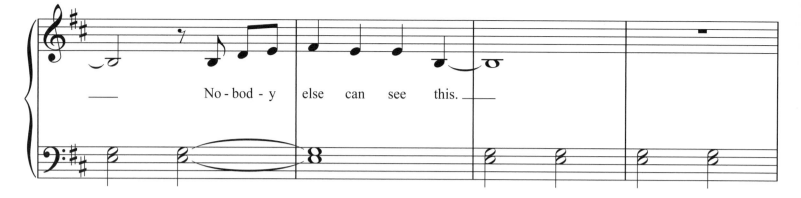

No - bod - y   else   can   see   this.

Bm

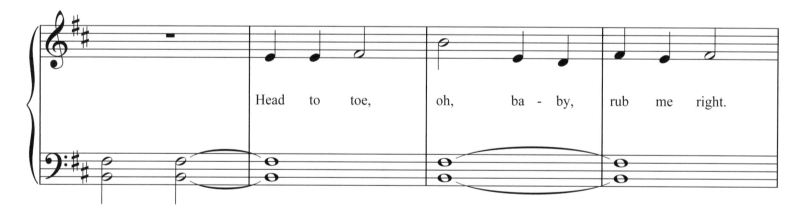

So   watch   and   learn,   I   won't   show   you   twice.

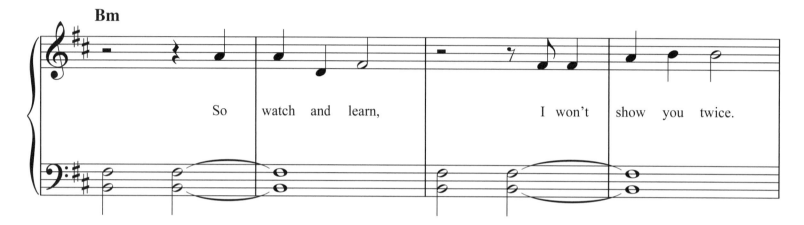

Head   to   toe,   oh,   ba - by,   rub   me   right.

Em7

But   if   I   share   my   se - cret,   you're   gon - na

have to keep it. _____ No - bod - y else can see this, _____

D.S. al Coda

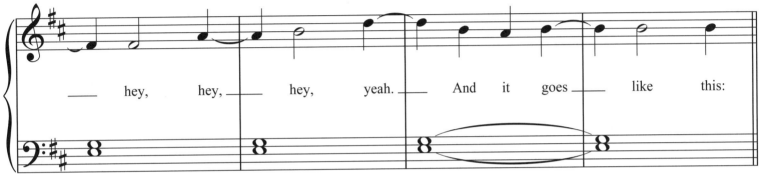

_____ hey, hey, _____ hey, yeah. _____ And it goes _____ like this:

CODA

moves. _____ like Jag - ger.

Bm

ONE MORE NIGHT

Words and Music by ADAM LEVINE,
JOHAN SCHUSTER and MAX MARTIN

Moderate groove

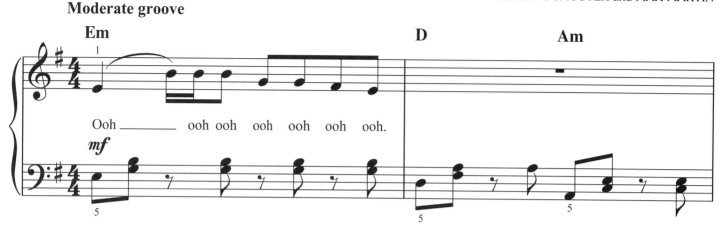

Ooh _____ ooh ooh ooh ooh ooh ooh.

Ooh _____ ooh ooh ooh ooh ooh ooh.   You and I go

hard   at each oth - er like we're   go - ing to war. __ You and I go
"no,"   but my bod - y keeps on   tell - ing you, "yes." __ Try to tell you,

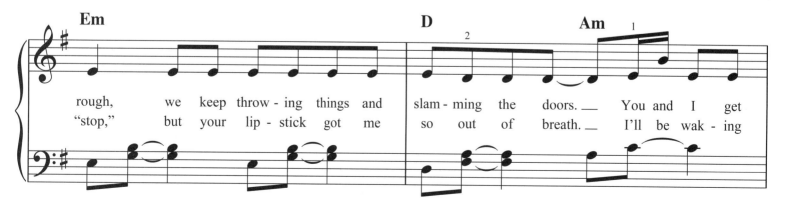

rough,   we keep throw - ing things and   slam - ming the doors. __ You and I get
"stop,"   but your lip - stick got me   so out of breath. __ I'll be wak - ing

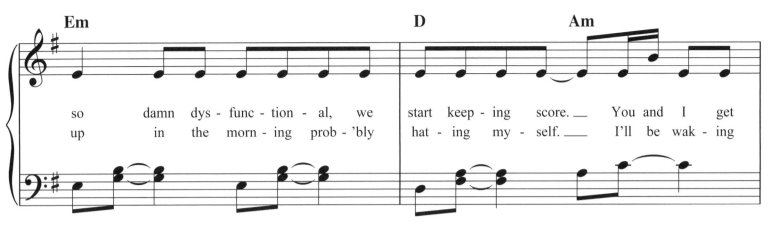

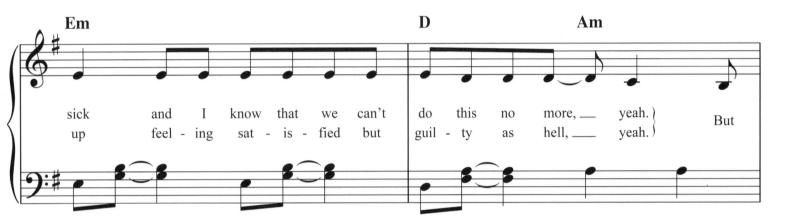

38

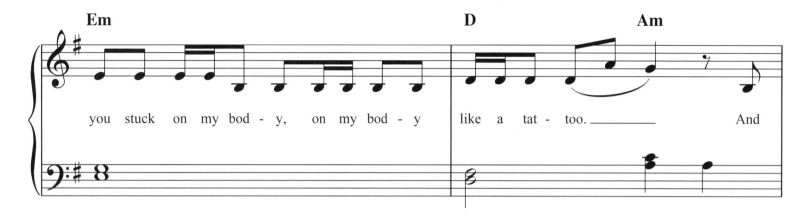

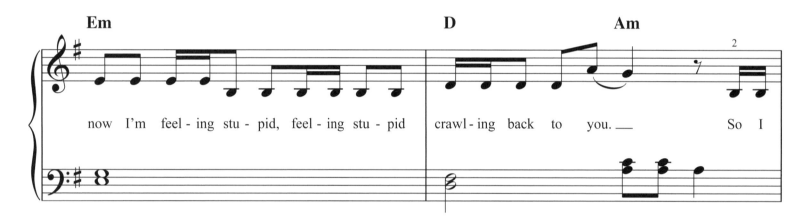

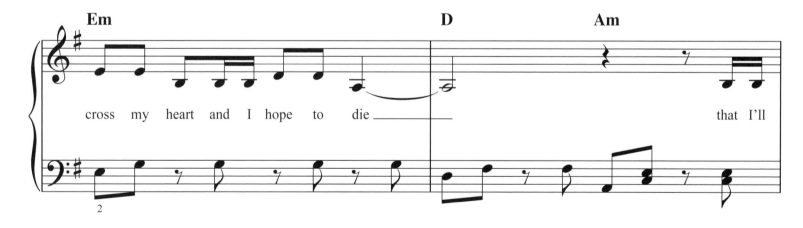

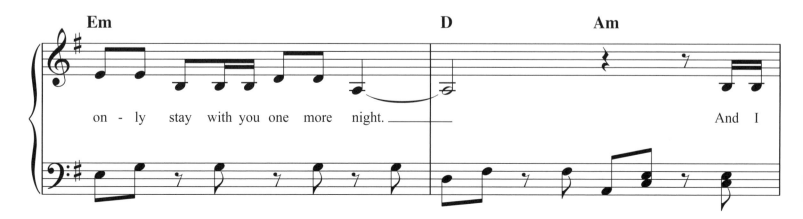

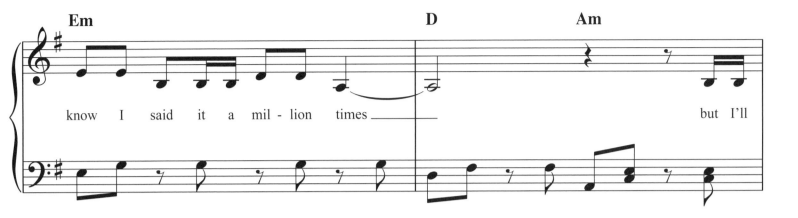

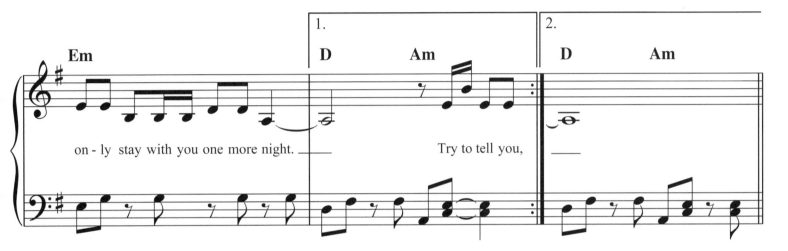

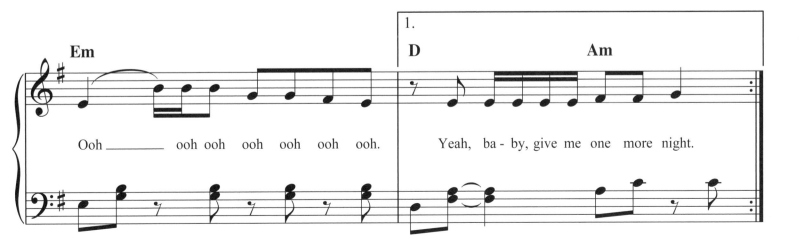

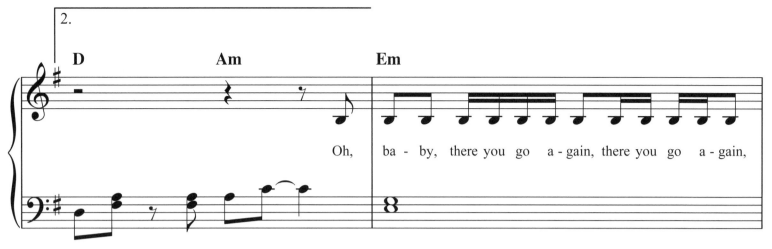

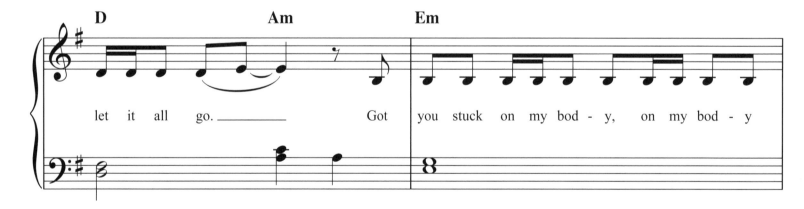

So I | cross my heart and I hope to die ___

that I'll | on-ly stay with you one more night. ___ | And I

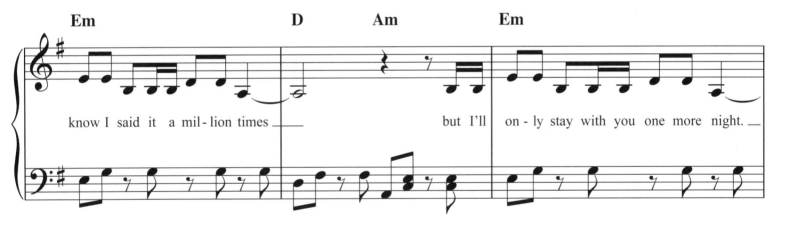

know I said it a mil-lion times ___ | but I'll | on-ly stay with you one more night. ___

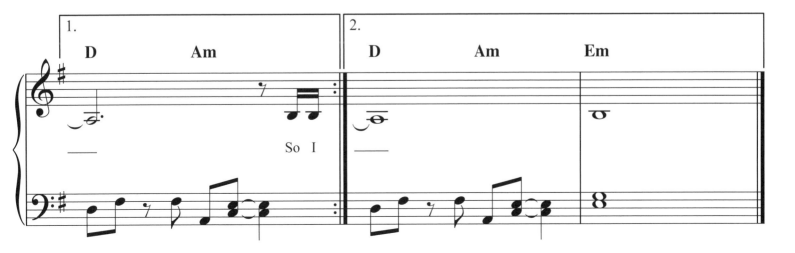

So I

SHE WILL BE LOVED

Words and Music by ADAM LEVINE
and JAMES VALENTINE

Moderately

Beau - ty queen of on - ly eigh - teen.
Tap on my win - dow, knock on my ___ door.

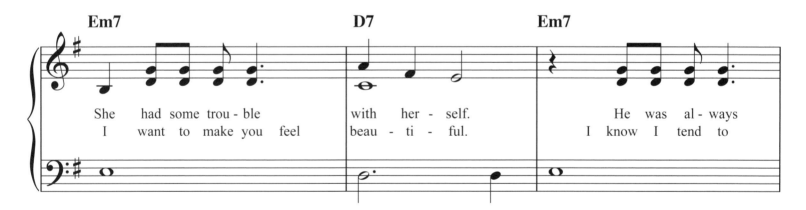

She had some trou - ble with her - self. He was al - ways
I want to make you feel beau - ti - ful. I know I tend to

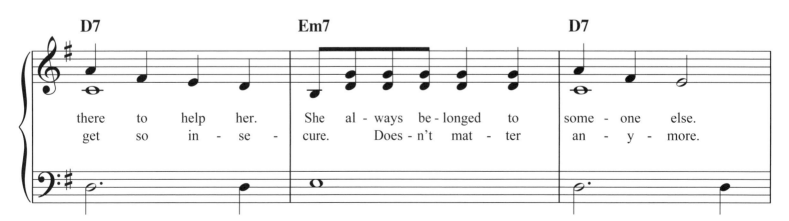

there to help her. She al - ways be - longed to some - one else.
get so in - se - cure. Does - n't mat - ter an - y - more.

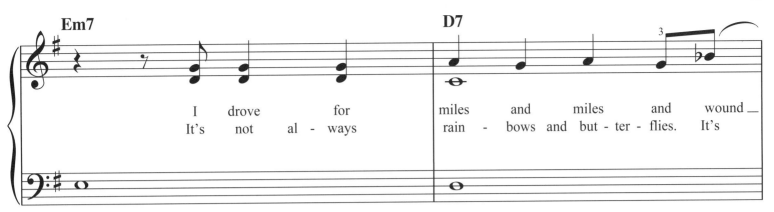

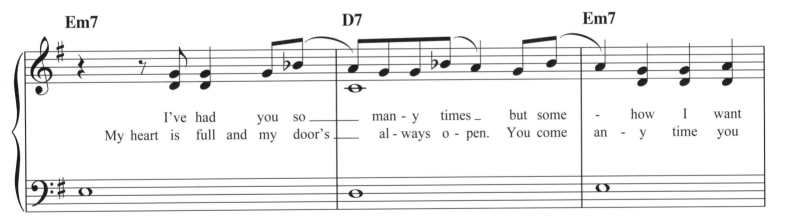

44

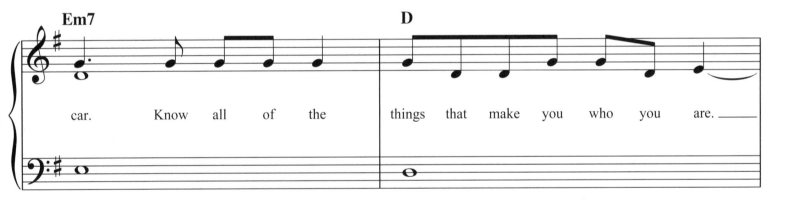

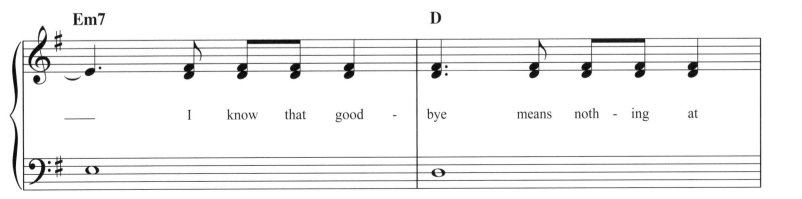

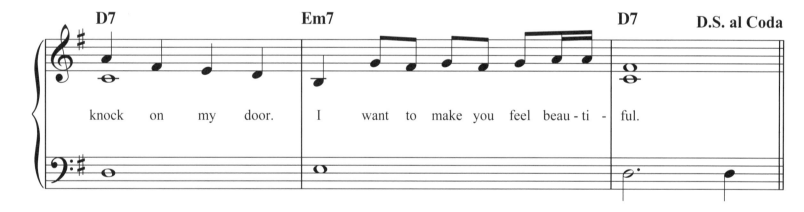

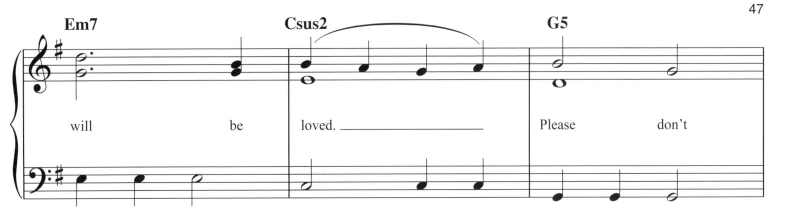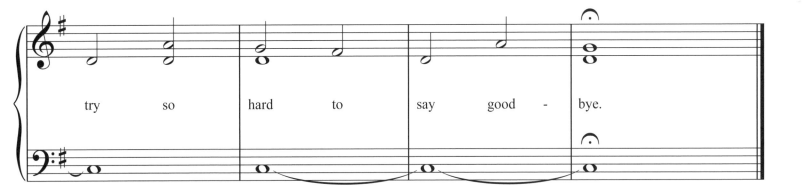

SUGAR

Words and Music by ADAM LEVINE, HENRY WALTER,
JOSHUA COLEMAN, LUKASZ GOTTWALD,
JACOB KASHER HINDLIN and MIKE POSNER

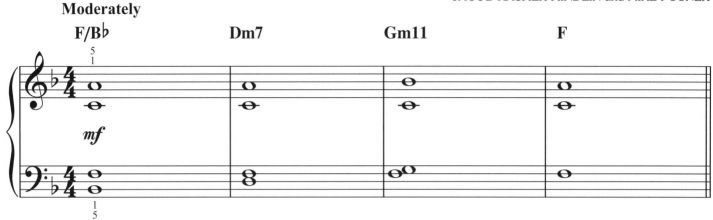

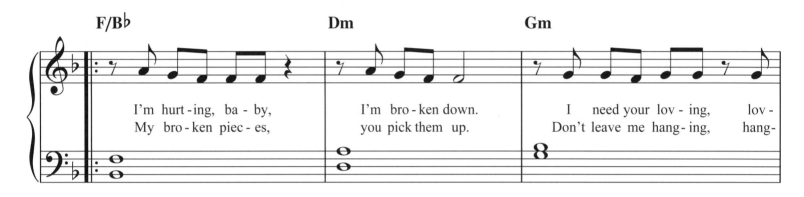

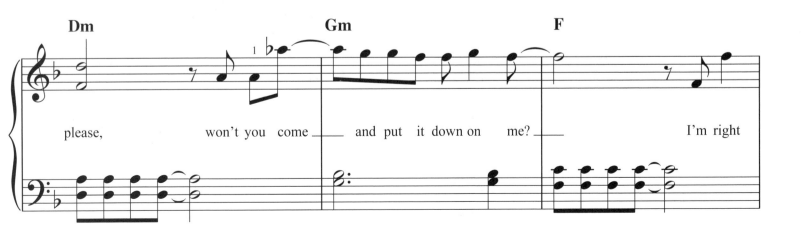

50

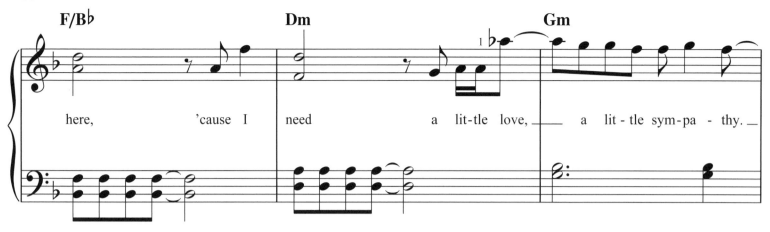

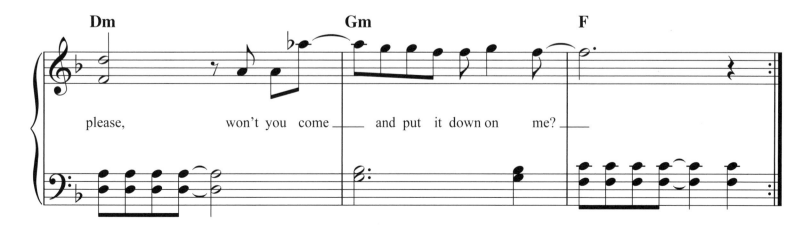

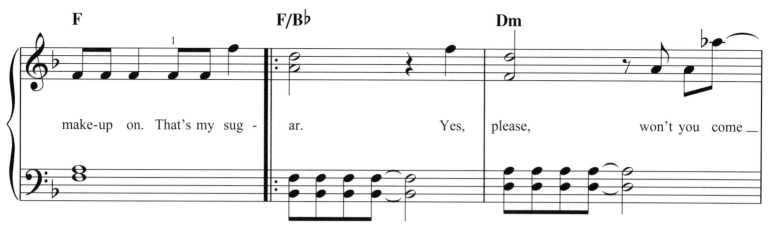

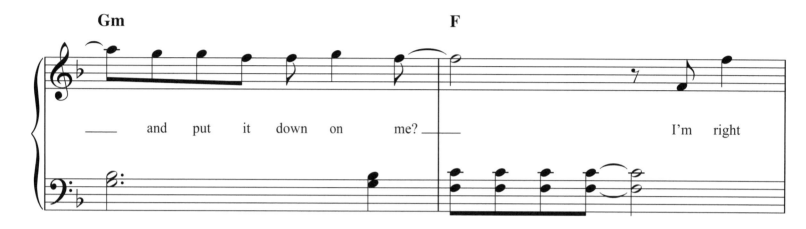

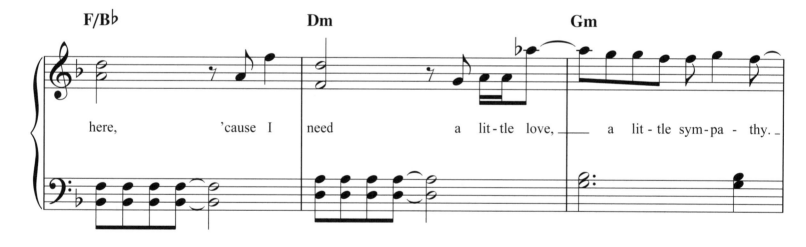

a lit - tle sweet - ness in my life. ___ You're sug -

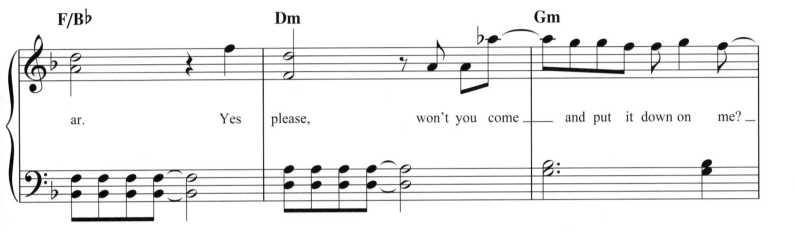

ar. Yes please, won't you come ___ and put it down on me? ___

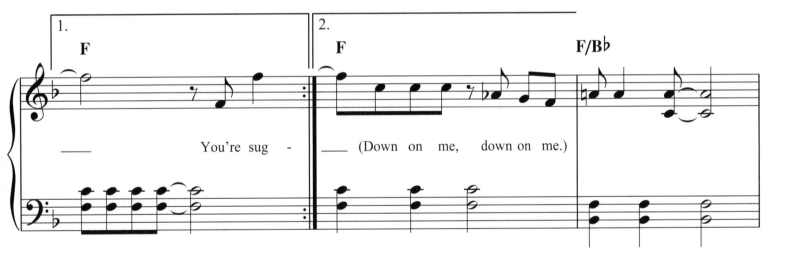

1.
___ You're sug -

2.
___ (Down on me, down on me.)

SUNDAY MORNING

Words and Music by ADAM LEVINE
and JESSE CARMICHAEL

Moderate groove

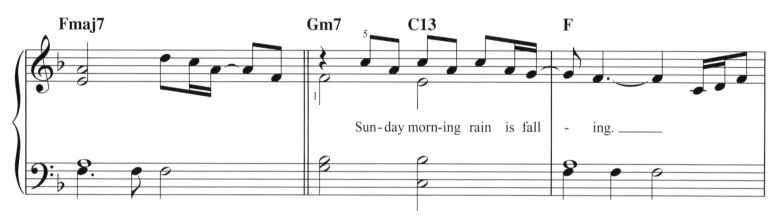

Sun-day morn-ing rain is fall - ing. ____

Steal some cov-ers, share some skin. ____   I like that. ____   Clouds are shroud-ing us ____ in

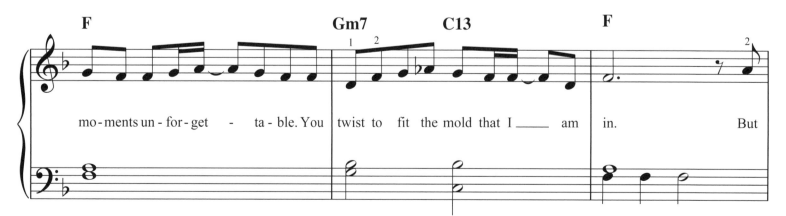

mo-ments un-for-get - ta-ble. You twist to fit the mold that I ____ am in.   But

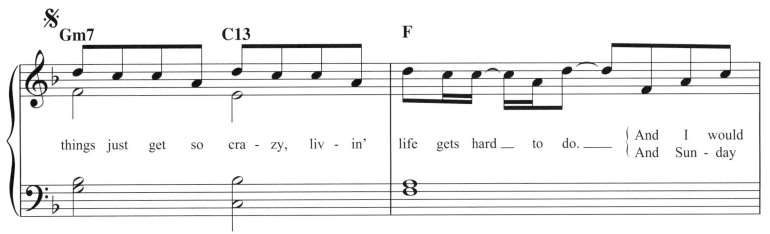

things just get so cra - zy, liv - in' life gets hard __ to do. ___ { And I would / And Sun - day

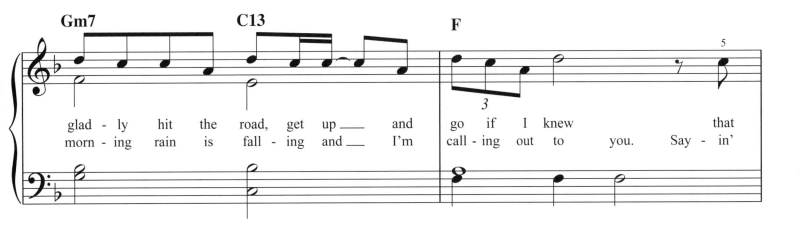

glad - ly hit the road, get up __ and go if I knew that
morn - ing rain is fall - ing and __ I'm call - ing out to you. Say - in'

some - day it would lead me back to you. ___ That
some - day it will bring me back to you. ___ Find a

some - day it would lead me back __ to you. That may be }
way to bring my - self back home __ to you. May not know, that may be }

all   I   need.   In   dark-ness she ___ is   all   I

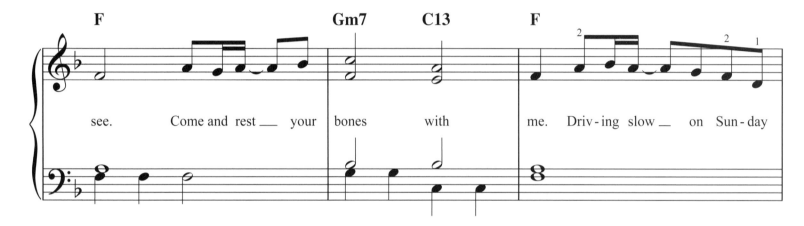

see.   Come and rest ___ your   bones   with   me.   Driv-ing slow ___ on   Sun-day

To Coda ⊕

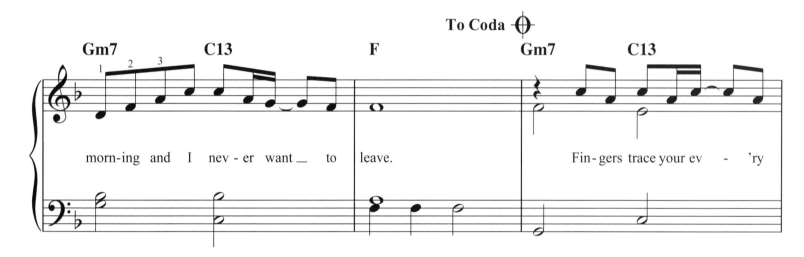

morn-ing   and   I   nev-er   want ___ to   leave.   Fin-gers trace your ev   -   'ry

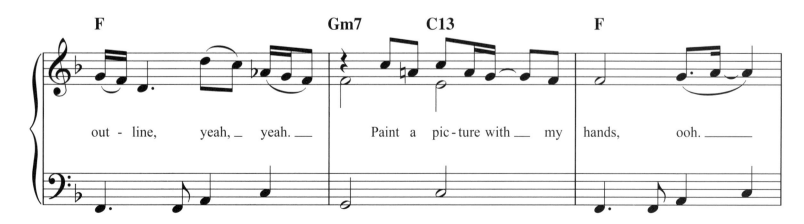

out - line,   yeah, ___ yeah. ___   Paint   a   pic-ture with ___ my   hands,   ooh. _____

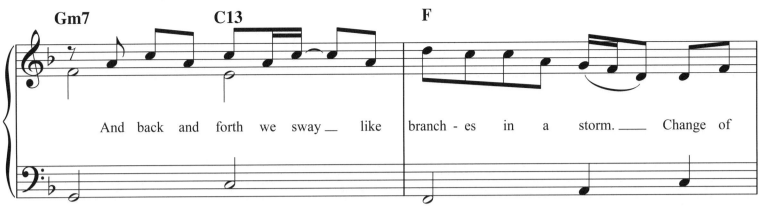

And back and forth we sway___ like branch-es in a storm.___ Change of

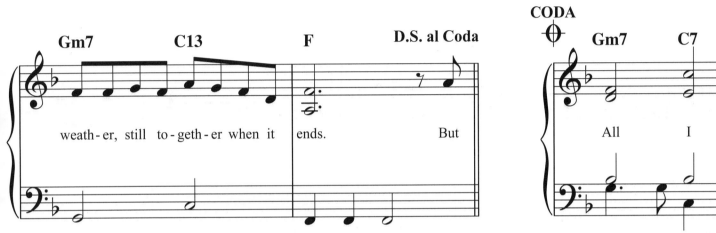

weath-er, still to-geth-er when it ends. But

CODA

All I

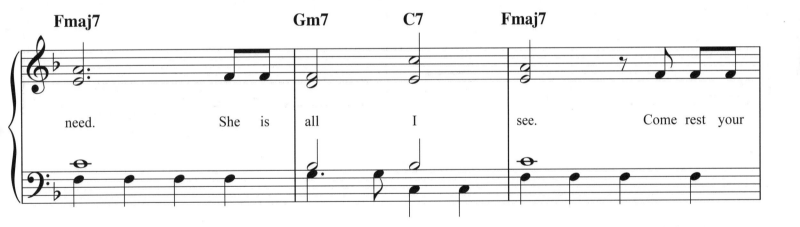

need. She is all I see. Come rest your

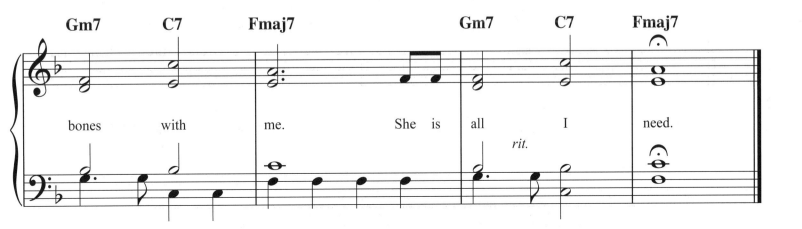

bones with me. She is all I need.

rit.

THIS LOVE

Words and Music by ADAM LEVINE
and JESSE CARMICHAEL

I was so high I did not rec-og-nize ___ the fire burn-ing

I tried my best to feed her ap-pe-tite, ___ keep her com-ing

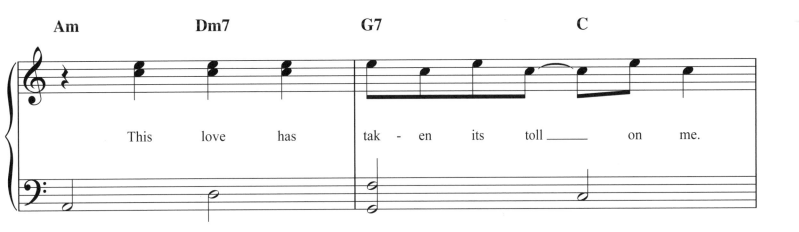

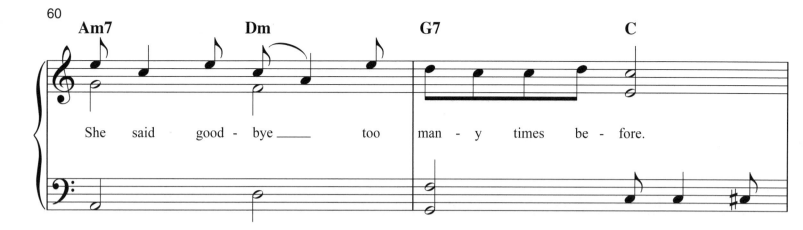

She said good-bye ____ too man-y times be-fore.

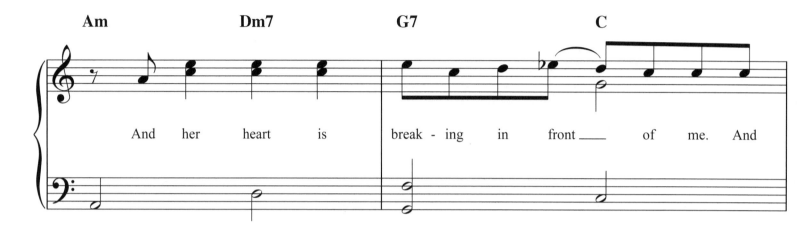

And her heart is break-ing in front ____ of me. And

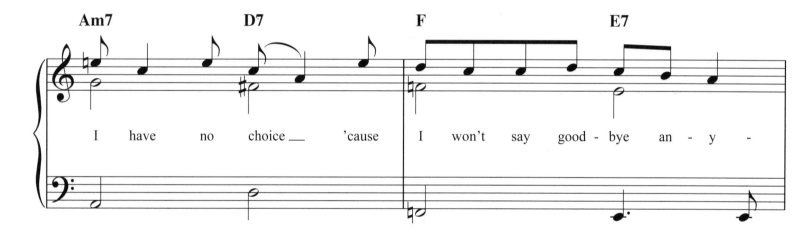

I have no choice ____ 'cause I won't say good-bye an-y -

more, whoa, ____ whoa, ____

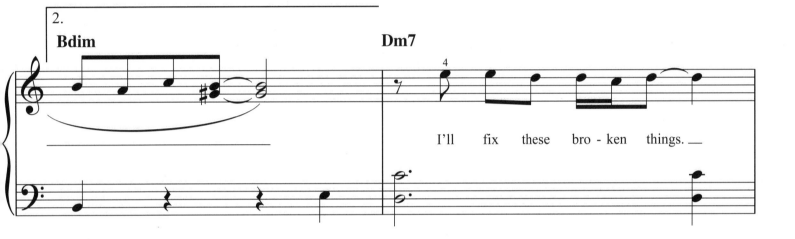

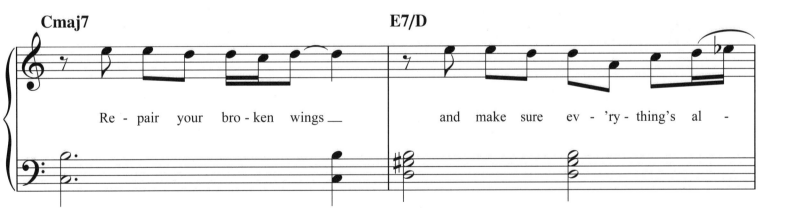

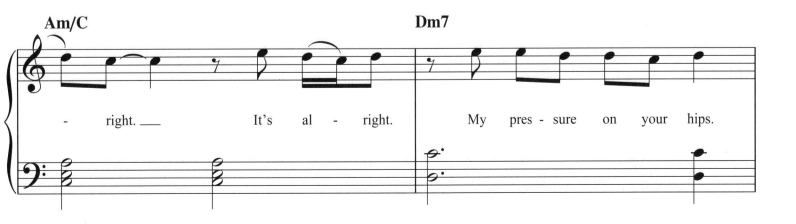

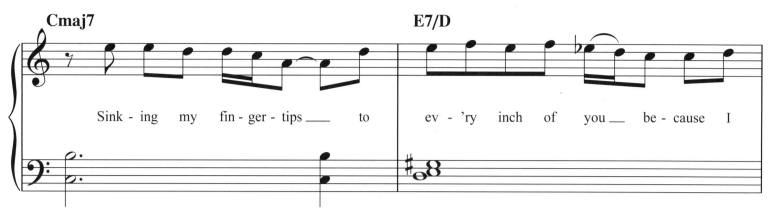

Cmaj7   E7/D

Sink - ing my fin - ger - tips ___ to   ev - 'ry inch of you ___ be - cause I

                                                    Am   Dm7

know that's what you want me to ___ do.   This   love   has
                                           This   love   has

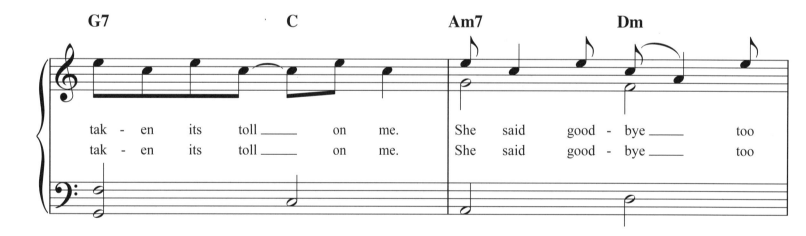

G7   C   Am7   Dm

tak - en its toll ___ on me.   She said good - bye ___ too
tak - en its toll ___ on me.   She said good - bye ___ too

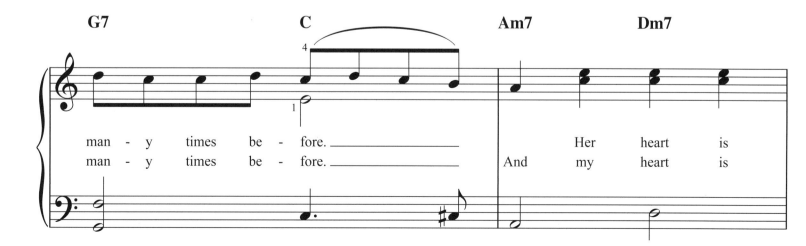

G7   C   Am7   Dm7

man - y times be - fore. ___   Her   heart   is
man - y times be - fore. ___   And   my   heart   is

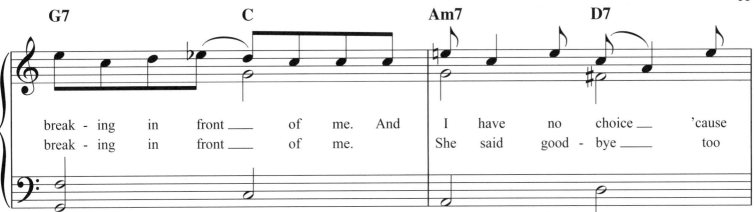

WON'T GO HOME WITHOUT YOU

Words and Music by
ADAM LEVINE

Moderate Rock

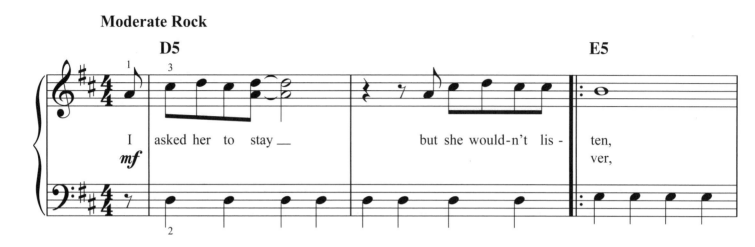

I asked her to stay ___ but she would-n't lis - ten, ver,

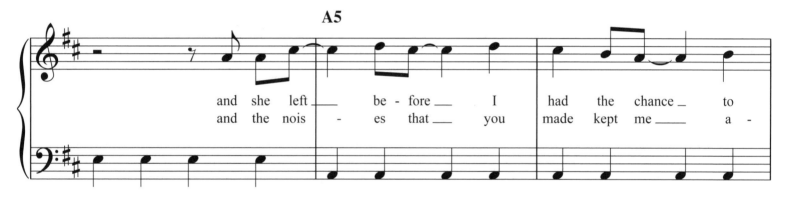

and she left ___ be - fore ___ I had the chance ___ to
and the nois - es that ___ you made kept me ___ a -

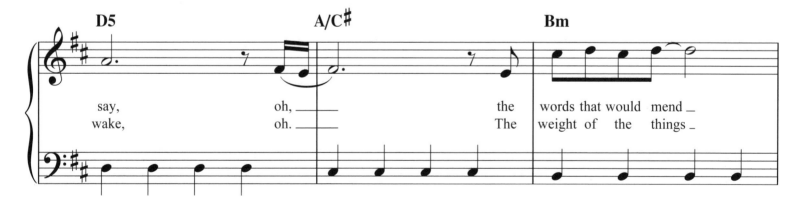

say, oh, ___ the words that would mend ___
wake, oh. ___ The weight of the things ___

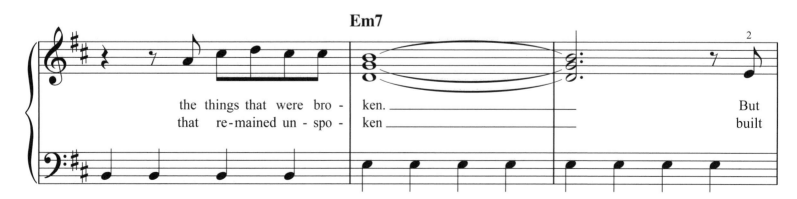

the things that were bro - ken. ___ But
that re - mained un - spo - ken ___ built

now it's far ___ too late, she's gone ___ a - way.
up so much ___ it crushed us ev - 'ry day.

Ev -'ry night you cry your - self to sleep, ___ think-ing why does this hap -

pen to me, ___ why does ev -'ry mo - ment have to be ___ so hard?

Hard to be - lieve that: It's not o - ver to - night, ___ just give me one more

To Coda ⊕

chance to make __ it right. I may not make it through the night, __ I

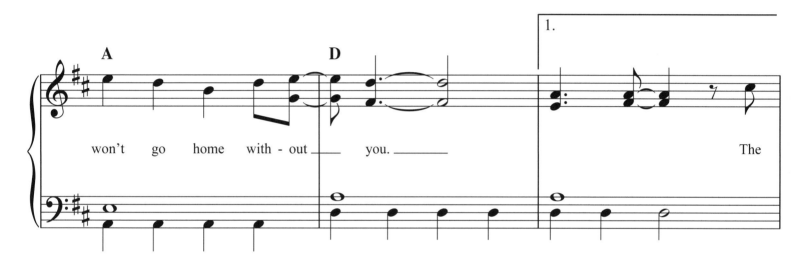

1.

won't go home with - out __ you. __ The

2.

taste of your breath, __ I'll nev - er get o - Oh. __

Of all the things I've felt __ but nev - er real - ly

shown, per - haps the worst is that ___ I ev - er let ___ you

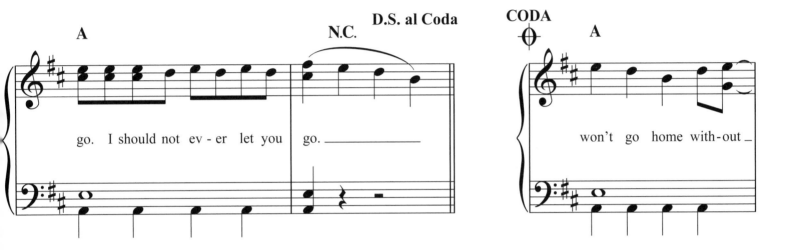

D.S. al Coda

N.C.

CODA

go. I should not ev - er let you go. _____

won't go home with-out ___

___ you. And I won't go home with - out ___ you, and I

won't go home with-out ___ you, and I won't go home with-out ___ you. ___

WAKE UP CALL

Words and Music by ADAM LEVINE
and JAMES VALENTINE

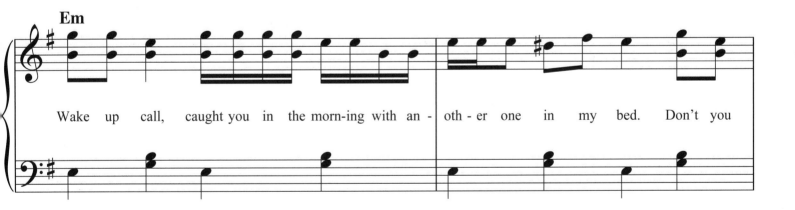

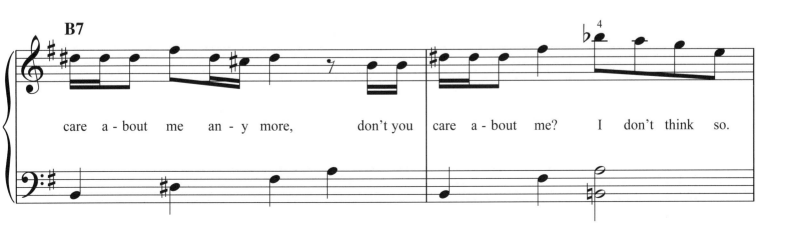

Six foot tall, came with-out a warn-ing so I had to shoot him dead. He won't

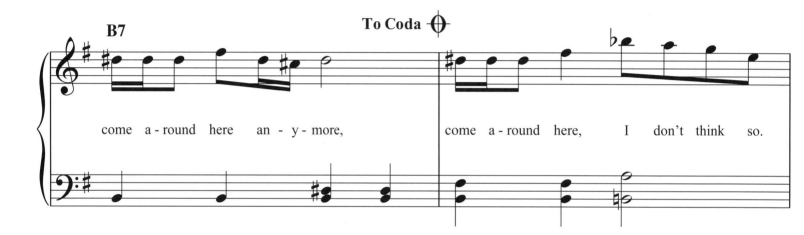

come a-round here an-y-more, come a-round here, I don't think so.

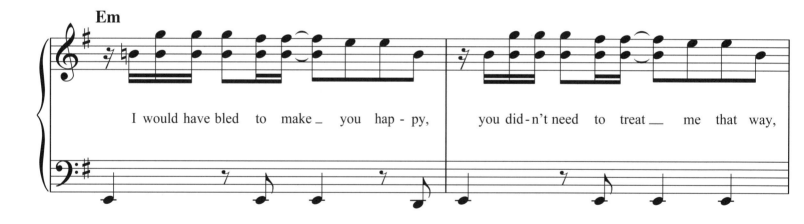

I would have bled to make _ you hap-py, you did-n't need to treat _ me that way,

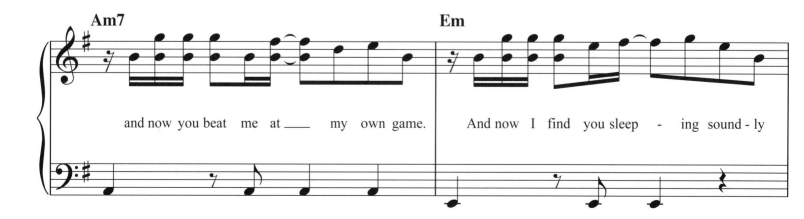

and now you beat me at _ my own game. And now I find you sleep - ing sound-ly

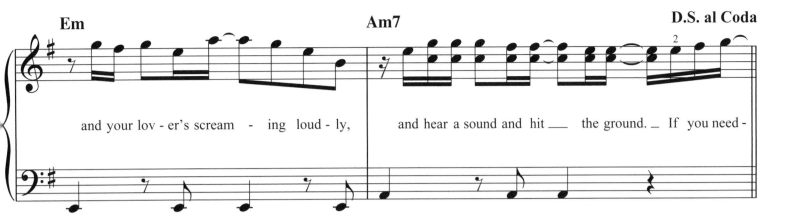

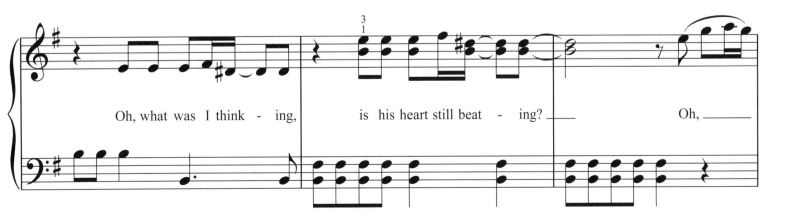

wake up call, caught you in the morn-ing with an - oth-er one in my bed. Don't you

care a - bout me an - y more, don't you care a - bout me? I don't think so.

Six foot tall, came with-out a warn-ing so I had to shoot him dead. He won't

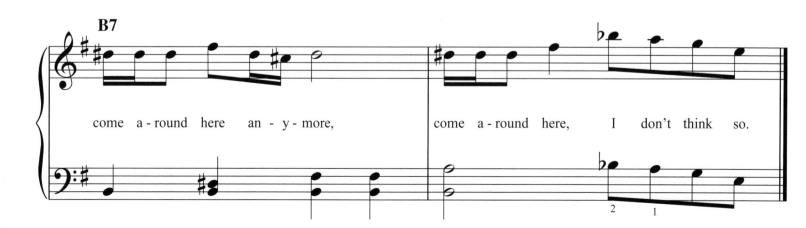

come a - round here an - y - more, come a - round here, I don't think so.